Being Present
to the Divine

Richard MacKay

EARTH PLEDGE

I pledge allegiance to the Earth
And all its sacred parts,
Its water, land, and living things
And all its human hearts.

I pledge allegiance to all life
And promise I shall care
To love and share all its gifts
With people everywhere

Anonymous

ACKNOWLEDGEMENTS

There is so much to acknowledge about the journey of this book, from the inception of the images to the publication. Perhaps a poem would say it better, lest I in all probability leave someone or something out. Through the talent of my expressive being, I can gratefully express this consciousness of the co-creative nature of Mother Earth.

I have experienced a rich forum of poetic sharing with the Huntsville Literary Association Poets group administered by Jimmy Robinson. From the Hi Noon Toastmaster's, especially Beverly Jones-Durr, I have developed my expressive speaking tools. I have found tools for artistic creative expression and catharsis through Lucia Capacchione's creative journal, my relationship with Linda Frank, and with others. With the helpful coaching of Tigrilla Gardenia and the music of the plants, I have seen how the consciousness of plants and animals contributes to our Spirituality and our Earth consciousness.

Through affiliation with Unity and the Center for Spiritual Living, I have found spirit guides, Wanda Gail Campbell, Dean Isley, Carol Landry, and David Leonard, towards an inclusive spirituality. Through my connection to the Interior Mythos website, I have seen the need for articulation of our spiritual heritage in contemporary consciousness.

Finally, I want to acknowledge all my Facebook friends in the Facebook poetry group, especially the founding members of EARTHSONG POETRY that I am administering. We all have shared our hearts poetically, artistically, and thoughtfully with what has touched our connection and action with nature, plants, animals, and Mother Earth.

Preface

EARTHSONG – INTIMACY WITH THE EARTH

"Our challenge is to create a new language, even a new sense of what it is to be human. It is to transcend not only national limitations, but even our species isolation, to enter into the larger community of living species. This brings about a completely new sense of reality and value." (Thomas Berry, "The Ecological Age," in The Dream of the Earth, 42).

AFTER A THUNDERSTORM

I'm sitting looking at the trees after a long, vibrant thunderstorm; I am contemplating my thoughts of all the mystery in this event.

THE LIMITS OF OUR CONSCIOUS PERCEPTIONS

We think of the environment through the filter of our own limited conscious perceptions. What if there is much more to the Earth than is obvious. Thinking that's all there is, what if there is more to all the plant and animal life than we see at casual glance?

ARE OTHER LIFE FORMS IN THE ENVIRONMENT DISCREETLY SEPARATE FROM US?

"Our relationship with the earth involves something more than pragmatic use, academic understanding, or aesthetic appreciation. A truly human intimacy with the earth and with the entire natural world is needed. Our children should be properly introduced to the world in which they live." (Thomas Berry, "Human Presence," in The Dream of the Earth, 13).

We think of other life forms as separate, discreet events from us; we don't see them as part of a greater oneness and mystery, which is beyond our five senses. There are questions: do life forms communicate in their own ways, perhaps energetically, that we can't perceive within the parameters of our closed off senses? Perhaps in our evolutionary space in time, there are many things in the environment that are much more mysterious and complex than many of us can fathom.

BEING IN HARMONY WITH THE DIVINE

If I just sit with this mystery in contemplative silence and let it speak to me in its own languages other than my own, then I can feel and be present to this "Peace that passes [my] understanding." I can feel this intimacy that I call the **Earthsong**. I can be present and feel in harmony with what I call the Divine.

In beauty may I walk.
all day long may I walk.
Through the returning seasons may I walk.

Beautifully will I possess again.
Beautifully birds…
Beautifully joyful birds…

On the trail marked with pollen may I walk.
With grasshoppers about my feet may I walk.
With dew about my feet may I walk.

With beauty may I walk.
With beauty before me may I walk
With beauty behind me may I walk.
With beauty above me may I walk
With beauty all around me may I walk.

In old age wandering on a trail of beauty, lively, may I walk.
In old age wandering on a trail of beauty, living again,
May I walk.

It is finished in beauty.

- Navajo Night Chant

"Your entire life is a curriculum. Everything you've got on your plate is where the stuff for your enlightenment is. It's breathtaking when you see the beauty of this design."   Ram Dass

TABLE OF CONTENTS

1 RHYTHMS AND RITUALS

Song of a Vision in the wilderness

1 The colors of evening, now color the sky
Signal of passage to night
and the hills in the distance, silhouette and fire,
sundown's now radiance of light.

CHORUS: Rhythms and rituals, now, life all around
Sharing our lives with the Earth.

2 The colors of the city, now, light up the night,
viewing from mountain on high,
The buildings, the people, their daytime jobs done
Merge in the stillness and flow into One.

Passage of time/ now/ feelings inside
Forever flowing within,
Expansion of ecstasy/ now/ moments in time
Great Mystery in all our lives.

3 We're coming together, now, evening's embrace
sharing our feelings, our day –
It's a game - it's a dance - it's a sharing of time -
it's a rhyming, a ritual, and it's yours and it's mine

CHORUS: These rhythms and rituals, now, all in our lives,
Sharing our life with each other –

4 Time is now bending, journey of dream
Voyage to distance of stars
Wonder of universe – Earth rising up,
brightens the view from afar

Repeat 1st verse and chorus

2 It's Only Rain

It rained all day
and into the night.
The wind was fierce,
it seemed to moan,
and the flags outside
were whipping around.

All this rain:
is it Mother Earth crying
when she is loving us
with so much blessing?

Is she crying over
how we're losing interest
in being her stewards?

Are we wanting rather to explore
the unknown desert out there
in our universe?

Is she crying
or am I only imagining?

Because, get real,
It's only rain.

3 Evening Wilderness

"Wilderness is not a luxury,
but a necessity of the Human Spirit."

Slight of wind caressing
pond's surface,
crystal ice sheet
frozen water
sculpted to stillness
in waves and patterns.
by the sweeping wind,
days and nights of cold.

In the distance,
see setting orb of sun
on top of horizontal
outline of trees.
Momentarily now,
look directly
at sun's brilliance.

Realize this tranquility
of space and time
in this wilderness.

The sun's orb sits now
on the horizon
slowly disappearing
in a majestic brilliance of color.
I sit in rapture
and listen to this
still inner voice:
"Hold here another minute."

The Universe, God,
the Mystery of life
has touched me
with this frozen pond surface,
the changing color and light,
the caressing feel of wind,
this wilderness,
and all the mystery
of evening.

4 EARTHDAY WHAT IFS

What if we could all
imagine a new spirit
story of harmony
in our thinking, our relationships,
and our actions
for Mother Earth.

What if I imagined
myself not just a solitary traveler
but part of a symphony
of the Earth.

What if in an unknown score,
I had my notes,
chords, melody, timbre
to play
in the harmony, health,
dance, and rhythm
of Life around me.

What if my individual
being was one puzzle piece
in my choices of connection,
and expansiveness or contraction.

What if a Dream of
Earth harmony was
effected by my thoughts,
actions, and love.

What if I am living
and loving in the dawning
of every new day
of a new Heaven and
a new Earth.

ON THE PURPOSE OF ART

The Navajos have a saying
that the purpose of art is
"to beautify the world."

On the face of it,
this does not sound so
different from the function
of art in the West. Yet,
pleasure for the senses is
only one dimension,
and by no means the most important,
of what Navajos understand
by making the world beautiful.

Beauty, rather, means balance,
the proper order of things.
Its affirmation or its restoration
implies that society,
the natural and the supernatural
environment, and the individual
are in the normal state of health
and harmony.

****Many works [therefore] of the first Americans express
and convey magic and mystery as much as beauty**

**<u>Teachings from the American Earth</u> – Indian Religion and Philosophy
Edited by Dennis and Barbara Tedlock**

5 THE RESONANCE OF TREES

~Remembering my Inner Shaman

The resonance of trees
sensual feeling of the breeze
a time frame slower than
my senses can perceive.

There's this unseen hum, now
near my inner ear
something I can hardly sense,
it seems so distinct and clear.

All around these miracles
beyond the limits of my senses
as I try to know the sense of it
within my own so small lens -

but this resonance of trees today
inviting me to share,
to take my animated presence
where the trees cannot dare.

To feel within this resonance
1,000 images passing me by.

So, I set the metronome
so very very low.
this resonance and
so slow drum beat,
so much lower
than I know.

Is it real?
Ask the trees
if this is so -

This resonance of trees
as I walk now with the breeze
in this time frame slower than
my senses can perceive.

6 Beside Still Waters

Chorus:
Oh, I sing my soul
Beside still waters
'Cause all that matters
is your loving heart,
is the song in your heart.

Oh, the me-lo-dy
from across the wind
Singing out in beauty
One beauty from within,
One voice, now, from within.

Interlude:
One beauty from within
One beauty from within
One beauty from within
One beauty from within

Share your loving heart
Reaching out in love
Harmony's vibrations
Share your song for all
Share your heart for all.

Oh, the church bells chime
Now, the church bells rhyme
It's your time to shine.
Let your light to shine.

7 At One – The Mountain

The mountain
absorbs people's language
heard from a distance,
and sounds merge in a tapestry
of murmurs and mutterings.

"It's just as well,"
I say to myself
as the hawk flies above,
Flying with the wind,
seeming free-flight
in widening arcs.

I enter the dialogue
space of vastness, and
merge with the various
silent rhythms and
shapes along the trail.

Occasional scurrying creatures
punctuate the wind's silence up here,
Reaching bushes and plants
sway slowly as if in water:
mesmerizing landscape,
Sea of Tranquility.

8 Pond Edge

Shimmering, rippling pond surface
mirror of reflections
encircling trees on edge.
-
An unexpected breeze gently spreads
a yellow-green mist of pollen
across the water's surface.

"Remain present here,"
says a voice inside.

Feeling at one, at peace,
Letting go of stresses and worries
Dragged down here
to pond's edge.

Feeling sense of renewal,
Seeing new hope.

9 MOUNTAIN HIGH

Sun to the West
white-yellow ball –

High precipice with
wind blowing across,
rushing like a
river rapids –

Colors turning to
cinnamon, brown and
dark green and yellow
with points of red –

Lone pine stands
upon hill to the right
sensually bathing in
the rushing winds –

Snow has begun to
appear along the
trail to here –

And, I am here
feeling the mountain
high.

10 SYMPHONY OF LIFE

Life is a symphony of the senses.
When did you forget
to see, to feel the next wave
on the water,
to feel the wind swaying
the trees, blowing through your hair
or to take to the path
in the forest,
to watch a bird enjoying
the skyway or circling above?

Is your life limited
to a mechanical enclosure,
cordoned off from outside
and dedicated only
to reasons of economy?

Life, however, even here
in this enclosure
real or imagined
plays it's symphony to you
if you are experiencing
the timbre and rhythms
of the sounds,
the shades of colors,
the poetry beyond noise of words,
the dance of the wind.

The symphony is playing -
Be present and listen
in gratitude.

AN UNEXPLORED ENVIRONMENT
I am Wondering!

I happen to look up
at the blue sky and clouds,
recognizing I'm seeing this
blue dome from inside space,
this space on the ground,
rather than from outer space.

There is so much mystery
that maybe I don't explore
in my reality of the Earth.

11 OH, I HEAR GOD'S VOICE

On witnessing myself in the Oneness of all creation

<u>Chorus:</u>

**Oh, I hear God's voice
in the setting sun,
in the cricket's song
We-are-all One.**

**In the rising sun
and the rising Earth
Oh, all these feelings
What are they worth?**

**2 Oh, I hear God's voice
in the wind and rain
in the rising sun
in this brand new day.**

**4 Oh, I hear God's voice
within my visions
in love and care
in a loving mission.**

12 EARTHRISE

Did you see
the Earthrise this morning?
Or was it this evening?

Of course you didn't see it.
It's a visual image
in my mind's eye
like a burning bush,
a musical song
in the silence,
an angelic harbinger
for a new story
in my heart.

Earthrise,
an image sent from Source.
An image sent from God
to remind me
we live in the universe?

We all live
in one sacred home.
If you can imagine it;
Mother Earth has declared
it's our home.

How will I treat my
brothers and sisters?
How will I treat myself?

Earthrise.

"Look at that picture over there! Here's the Earth coming up.
Wow, is that pretty!"

–William Anders, Apollo 8, December 24, 1968

NOTES

"Tell me a story, a story that will be my story as well as the story of everyone and everything about me, the story that brings us together in a valley community, a story that brings together the human community with every living being in the valley, a story that brings us together under the arc of the great blue sky in the day and the starry heavens at night, a story that will drench us with rain and dry us in the wind, a story told by humans to one another that will also be the story that the wood thrush sings in the thicket, the story that the river recites in its downward journey, the story that Storm King Mountain images forth in the fullness of its grandeur."

— Thomas Berry, - The Dream of the Earth